# Love & Existentialism

Amelia Michels

BookLeaf Publishing

India | USA | UK

Presentation by *BookLeaf Publishing*

Web: www.bookleafpub.com

E-mail: info@bookleafpub.com

ISBN: 978-93-5744-329-6

First edition 2022

# DEDICATION

*To you,*

*for me*

# PREFACE

To write is to cut open your soul & let it bleed
with conviction
I am an open book if you just ask
but to openly tell without ever being asked  how
could I demand such attention
The inner critic venomously begs for me to be
silent
to share with you my words becomes an act of
defiance
so
dear reader,
be kind
always be kind
Enjoy my chaotic voice
clandestinely romanticised storytelling
and existential complex

I appreciate you

# Tempest storm

We can't turn our back and wait for the sun to
shine
there's no time to draw the line
Between love and fear
between who we are and who we wish to be
The end is drawing in near as
ten floods leak from my lashes
as the last cloud drains away
We are mere splashes in a world where the
ocean does not wait to swallow
us up
Desperate to create a wave that the world will
see
but It is impossible to be
more than the sea
of a million more droplets
Why is not being me
just me
more than enough
for the tempest storm to surge and roar
but I see,
the world can not hear me through all of this
thunder
only a loud silence

How does one become a tornado
to erupt like a volcano
Etching towards the journey's end, inspiring to
touch all those around
If the world will not stand still and seek another
sound

How do you be seen as a tempest storm in a
world filled with hurricanes?

# Fateless love

Lovers always find a way, it is unmistakably so
in the movies
In real life, love can become finite
The romance genre is outcrying in dismay at the
end of this story
Reality is not sorry for breaking our hearts
and moving on from the pieces without a second
start
Desperate confidence to do another take
just one more take
we can make it right
at least for my sake
Is the movie worth making if we can't keep
creating
the love we had found
Profound we were, a drowned prospect we
became
Now with only dust to show
left to pick up the remains
A cheated desire without the end take
A fragment of a sentence left unread

Isn't it pretty to think that we could have been
something?

Isn't it pretty to think that we ever were in the
first place?

A fateful love but which was not made to
conquer fate

# Remember my name

5

My biggest fear is being unremarkable
I say this with utmost candor
to leave without creating an eternal ember
What is the answer
to this burning need to imprint
An Unconscious testimony
of this constant symphony
Remember my name
Remember my name
What does it take to earn
a mark in history's Hall of fame
Such a Short span to play the waiting game
Tick Tock
Existential crisis
Or an everyday existentialist
It's all the same
Remember my name

# Love legacy

If you are known for anything
during your time on earth
Let it be for all the love you gave
And all the love you accepted
The depths of your love will be your legacy
as perhaps the shallowness of your love will
haunt you

# Unsaid words

I have a thousand things to say to you
and a thousand reasons not to
but one reason that I did,
one word to explain why
regret

Unsaid words are a death sentence
slow suffocating demise
Clawing at your throat as you take your last
breath
as are all the things you never let yourself try
Your legs beg for once last run right just as they
give out
Final bittersweet moments without the sweetness

There is shame in speaking words some would
say were better left unsaid
as if we have eternity to let the regret boil over
What they don't know can't hurt them
but what they don't know, will hurt the both of
you
Feelings were made to be expressed not bottled
up and made oppressed

There is wasted time in regretting what has
already been said
At least I cannot regret what so many of us do
To leave words unsaid and to do die knowing
they never knew

# Chronic seeker

I often wonder about my place in this world
Countless opposing desires, faiths rooted in
truths unknown
Where do I belong?
Is the path laid out before me, or shall I pave it
alone?
Each step I pray is guiding me towards my
divine calling
but I can't help to wonder,
Again
is my existence seamlessly meaningless among
the galaxies?
Haven't these questions been pondered since the
beginning of time?
Never to be concluded with plausible answers
or did we just forget
where we came from
Magnetised energy shifting fates and healing
souls
Science, religion, universe, divine love
Human explanations for incomprehensible
glories
perhaps we should simply cease in the search
accept our fates as eternal

Then we could come to understand the beauty of
our morality
Life becomes all that more precious when only
given this one chance, on this one celestial plane
and yet, I still wonder
What is the meaning?

Asking questions in an answerless world

# Worthiness

An angel questions her worthiness of his love
Questions what she did to ever deserve this love
Truth is, this is all she ever did deserve and
failed to receive
Ironic, an angel to ever question such a thing

# Present nostalgia

Wine held delicately in my hand,
your electric fingers igniting the current of my
own skin
Can we stay like this forever?
With honey dripping from our essence,
while the moon shines the only light,
illuminating in fluorescence
I make a wish for eternity
I have only experienced love to be tragic
Never quite declared an epic love affair
Nevertheless, always magic
Somehow, I think you and I will mirror a
dramatic classic
The tornado inspiring fusion of both
Rising and falling all at once
I pause there, midway thought
Curled up in your lap
Our bodies remain tangled atoms dancing,
and our souls?
They are nostalgic for the now

The present moment portal

# To save you

The feeling of being stuck, beyond assistance
With not a single looming light to convey an exit
Not a single, able hand reaching down to save
you
Infinite blackness, consuming dampness
To enter your mind for only a day
Only then will I understand how to be that able,
stretched out hand,
Your saving grace
Liberating words would flow effortlessly from
my lips
And my arms would finally be enough to keep
you from yourself
I would befriend your emotions, decipher your
problems
Be you when you are too exhausted to breathe

I would take up my sword and travel to your
deepest, most forbidden caves
Siv through the void until I found a means of
destroying your attachments with the monsters
who live inside

I will burn through your mind until there is no
energy that conspires in your demise
If I am the only dry entity able to catch alight
You know damn well
I'd set myself ignite

To save a life

# Psychological symmetry

Warm my cold lifeless hands with your kisses
Resurrect my half beating heart with the blood
pounding in yours
Mend my mind with your chaotic words
A rare psychological symmetry
we have found
For It wasn't the first time that you touched me
but the first time you held me while I cried
From that date on
I belonged to you absolutely
The emotional intimacy of a fantasy
I live out with you in ecstasy
The intellectual intimacy of poet prose
I draw pen to paper and compose
The story of how you made me alter my
expectations of love
could give birth to a lifetime of tales
Details lay claim to a century-old romance
concrete until the pavement undermines
At least
my story holds more gravity with your spine
Until you and I
are obsolete

# Condition less

The notion of unconditional love is cast around
so frivolously
But what does it mean to love unconditionally?
Instead of being garnered minimally
Have I ever really felt it?
Love from another without a condition attached?
I love you until...
I love you now...
I love you but...
There was always an air of responsibility from
the love I earned
It was never said out loud enough to me for me
to believe that the love I received was indeed
free
What more can I achieve
until unconditional love becomes a guarantee
Not a one-way street
Seeing is believing
all I saw were conditions
filled with selfish ambitions
Until disappointment became
disassociation
From those who put a high price on the love to
which I wasn't given an invite

A love without an end sounds like
I love you even if...
I love you still…
I'll love you after all
and without ever knowing it
for myself
I still think I love you
limitlessly

# Love in motion

A whirlwind of emotions lace around me,
masquerading through my memories
everything I have ever felt, all those I have ever
loved
bursting at the seams with so little life to have
been lived
but a million lives I have led
a mountain of loves I have been enthralled by
reminiscent affections are freed each time a
name is mentioned
just one single name and I can tell you when I
knew there was no going back to before I had
met them
no past without them has power once we
collided
in one fail swoop, I can recall the feeling of
being touched by a hand that belongs only to
them
remember the way they said my name
like a song that remains in the back of my mind
anxious to be sung once again
what we once held
torments me still

love in motion is being taken by two hands of a
soul you know is yours forever
never to be lost and always yours to hold
to have and to hold for as long as love remains
in motion
whilst the universe exists, this notion carries true
once intertwined, our souls remain familiars
eternally woven
no matter the lengths we go to tear the
connection apart
it will outlive
even us
for it was during this breath of time
where we truly experienced
love in motion

# Are you happy?

Am I happy?
Are you happy?
Among the long nights, lavish paycheques, and
social media highlights
"Are you happy?"
They pause, taken aback
I watch as their eyes stare fixed ahead, internally
they are searching within for the answer
But are they happy?
When was the last time they felt genuine joy,
experienced bone-chattering laughter?
Does peace reside within their souls
permanently?
Or is autopilot their only gear?
Their eyes meet mine again, I give a reassuring
smile.
"I think so" they respond

But

Life isn't made to be felt halfway
Life is too short to be unsure

# Heal yourself

But who heals the healer?
I'm wrestling with accepting this label, to accept
responsibility
or reject it
Is my cup really overflowing with an abundance
of love?
or am I an energy field that is slowly being
vaporised and left lacking?
consequentially robbing myself
Then they leave, leaving me more drained than
before.
So tell me
who heals the healer?
I have been doing it all along
healing myself
getting back up
mending
recovering
I have dragged myself from the depths time and
time again
and still,
I have become a pitstop for the broken
Truth is, the real strength derives from filling
your own tank

I'm tired
please
become your own healer

# Self destruction

Self-destruction is used to describe addictions
like drug abuse and gambling.
Everything that is so painfully clear to outsiders'
eyes, looking in on a broken life.

But what about those who live so far within their
minds they can't admire all that is occurring
around them?
Doomed to destroy it all
When everything around you screams to be
appreciated, and you fail to do so, you can be
sure the good will make its way out of your life
Only for you to miss it when it's all gone.
I've been there, standing in the eye of my
childhood dream
pacing around the eternal city,
The way I had always imagined.
I was there, but not really,
lost in a sea of problems that didn't quite exist
My only regret is not cherishing those fleeting
moments I now lust over

I have learned that dwelling on the past and
obsessing about the future is a two-ingredient
recipe for self-destructing.
You are exactly where you've dreamt of being
So be here

# Love for all is my religion

I have lived in an Islamic nation, celebrating
their festivities.
For years, I surrounded myself around the
Christian community, quoting Jesus.
I have studied Buddhism and the ways of the
Dalai Lama.
Practices of New Age spirituality have made
their way into my heart

Existentialism is most present in my mind
After all this, I understand the answers I seek, I
may never find

I don't know if the answer is ceasing my Karma
Or to choose one path & completely restart
Against all other universal languages, love lives
within our hearts
Found within the small miracles of life
And colliding with compassion, exploding from
a stranger's eyes
This, I know

Religion has become a sort of fine art

Painting ancient manuscripts & interpreting the
written word
Changing within the worlds of ourselves
Fickle, and lost in translation
With so much fixation on rules & damnation
Identities blurred with masks worn for show

I think I know,
Love & acceptance is the only liberation

With love, sin lessens
With love, good deeds rise
With love, suffering is dulled
With love, connection to everything is
exemplified

The truth is universally recognisable, from each
culture to the next
Timeless among the millenniums

Grace is my practice
Love for all is my religion

"I belong to no religion. My religion is love.
Every heart is my temple." – Rumi

# Uncomfortability within the
comfort zone

We met, in the confines of classrooms and
friendship circles
for years we remained together, while I dreamt
for more than those four walls
nurturing my lust for life beyond everything I
had ever known
The countdown to our separation kept the
wildness within me,
daydreaming of stories, I would someday tell
My fingertips danced across atlas's instead of
textbooks
colouring in pastels, avoiding black and blue

and here you are, after spreading your wings
across the globe
scars afresh with memories
of desert dreams and European sunlight
home, at last, the fire within subsided

but

time moves fast
faster than you can

you've returned and so has the restlessness
within your own skin
happiness comes and goes
but the desire wears a permanent face
she whispers
"There is more for you elsewhere"
I search and search but am yet to find
Borders closing in, there is no time

Uncomfortability within the comfort zone
I once welcomed you within my home
During my younger years, you were free to roam
you boarded those planes with me
until I lived beyond my comfort zone

With discontentment, comes acceptance
I am learning that I am exactly where I need to
be
learning to be comfortable standing still
Allow me this time
I want to feel rested when I am resting

I don't need your aggravation to keep me on my
toes
I am slowing my run
appreciating the view on route to my destination
Run ahead
I don't need you anymore

I know you
you're afraid to slow down
to peer inside of yourself
afraid of what you might find
You search for the next distraction
but not me
not anymore
this will not be my way of life

I will dive so deep within myself
it will be uncomfortable
healing is uncomfortable
So I won't run, not anymore
This is my race

My breath has slowed
living gently within me
No rush
no place to be
but here

The past has proved beautiful, and the future is
just on the horizon
Yet to be here, is my greatest pleasure

I think I shall stay a while longer

# Quiet undoing

The feeling of hitting 'rock bottom' isn't always when everything in your life takes a very visible plummeting crash. I've seen it also in the form of a quiet undoing of your interior home. When your mind registers everything as "not quite right" while your heart knows that something needs to change. Your mind attempts to protect you, not wishing to send you into overdrive. But your heart knows. Your soul knows exactly what it wants. If only you would sit with yourself long enough to hear it whisper to you - what you already know.

# Beauty in the chaos

I can't tell you what it feels like for someone to
see the depths of your soul and decide it wasn't
for them.
But perhaps you already know what I describe.

They want to know so much about you, more
than you are willing to tell.
Persistence breeds surrender, and so you let
them see the broken parts in your heart and the
stubborn shatters within your soul.
They assure you,
it's all alluring, necessary to encapsulate your
chaotic beauty,
our darkness is one and the same.
Just to turn around and reject every single inch
of you.
Even the good, even the parts of you they swore
they couldn't live without.
Was everything they said only a lie? You
wonder.
Did I show too much of myself?

No.

They only did not have the strength to open the
space you needed
Please do not build back up your walls, and hide
the shadows deep within
Did this not at least, open your heart?
Keep it open.
Sometimes we need to be broken open to begin
transforming
Such as a butterfly cocoon is destroyed to bring
life to the wings of flight

Let your strength be the light

# The chase

I've pined insatiably for new loves, fresh
experiences, and unrequited flames
So much so, I do not know how to rest
To claim something that has been given to me
Unable to accept what is for me
without the need to persuade
The act of chasing seems to be innately in me
To chase the dreams, to chase the unrequited
flames
Not needing to fight for someone to want me or
for an experience to come my way
an unfamiliar phenomenon
only seen written in screenplays
I tire of everything I have ever desired
When will my need to persist finally retire

Once I have it
I almost, no longer want it

# A crossroads

The indescribable urge of wanting a reset
Ignorant
naive
foolish
they whisper
To make an impetuous decision to abandon one's
life
A turning point without explanation
making plans without a clear destination
My voice pipes up
"What is just one year, out of my long life?"
If in pursuit of adventure
a year transforms into an infinite collage of
dazzling memories
new faces to scrapbook
written words of stories I'll have to share
Much experience can be gifted in just one year
if given the freedom to do so
When home calls you back from across the seas
A year will be equivalent to a week for all those
you left behind
living in their vanilla houses
Their hours entail the same mundane
Different day, identical month

If frustration has become a primal feeling you
carry around
seeping in on your words, haunting your
demeanor
It's time to move forward
It's like walking on a lava-filled floor
weary not to step in the wrong direction
or you'll erupt
If daily you balance on the tipping end and often
jump right over
It's time to crossover

The most dreadful form of time pass is to remain
the unchanged
and wake up in the same place I was a year ago

www.ingramcontent.com/pod-product-compliance
Lightning Source LLC
Chambersburg PA
CBHW070613160726
48003CB00005B/2249